Sally Line
the complete story

Ferry Publications, PO Box 33, Ramsey, Isle of Man IM99 4LP
Tel: +44 (0) 1624 898445   Fax +44 (0) 1624 898449
Email: ferrypubs@aol.com   Website: www.ferrypubs.co.uk

Introduction

Ferry Publications' first published their Sally Line book in 1992. At that time the Company was riding high and in a buoyant mood following the jumboisation of the *Sally Sky*. But with the opening of the Channel Tunnel and improved standards on new ships on the Dover-Calais service by market leaders P&O European Ferries, the pendulum of Sally's fortunes swung dramatically.

The transfer of the long-established Ostend-Dover service to Ramsgate in 1994 brought little comfort and security to either Port Ramsgate or Sally Line. The later joint venture with Holyman was to prove disastrous for all concerned. The last ditch attempt by the restructuring of Sally Line, marketed as Sally Direct, was also to be short-lived.

It is ironic that the operator which was to replace Sally Line has mada modest success of its Ostend service and now Dunkerque West is once again establishing itself as an important ferry link with Dover as Norfolkline's operation shows every sign of early success.

This republished title updates the original publication written by Geoffrey Breeze in 1992. The updated and edited version includes both the workings of RMT and Holyman Sally so that an overall picture can be formed of Sally's operations until their sad demise in November 1998.

Miles Cowsill and John Hendy
June 2001

ACKNOWLEDGEMENTS

The authors are grateful for the assistance of Bill Moses with the production of this publication. They would also like to acknowledge the kind co-operation and assistance of Mike Louagie, Philippe Holthof, Chris Randall and FotoFlite.

The *Sally Sky* outward bound from Ramsgate in the revised livery introduced in 1997. *(FotoFlite)*

Foreword

To be given the opportunity to run Sally towards the end of 1995 was a challenge too good to miss. Moreover, it was a homecoming; my grandfather's boatyard had been located on the site of the present port and I was born in Ramsgate, spending much of my childhood messing about in boats in The Royal Marina.

Even before my appointment as Chief Executive, it was evident to me that without a significant repositioning of the business in the face of competition from the Tunnel, it would soon be too late. In the event my prognosis was closer to the truth than I had imagined as the previously loyal customer base was already being eroded. Wooed by a loss leader rate structure, the customers who had enthusiastically welcomed Sally as the new player on the Channel deserted the operation with equal haste.

So it was that 20 eventful years saw both the birth and death of a significant player on the short sea.

Sally Ferries, with its friendly red cartoon ferry trademark, was launched on the Channel offering a standard of service and facilities previously never seen south of Stockholm and the Baltic style smorgasbord offered in the restaurant became a legend. The company achieved record-breaking results, largely ignored by the traditional operators in Dover.

Over the years the Sally group had additional financial pressures, notably the need to invest in the expansion of Port Ramsgate, leased from Thanet District Council, and the idiosyncrasies of operating with both French and Belgian crews. However, the final blow came in the form of a price war as surface operators attempted to cling on to their share of the market in the face of what some saw as unfair competition from the Channel Tunnel. It is ironic that the demise of Sally was ultimately as a result of low-ticket prices, something that the Scandinavians had delivered to the Channel nearly 20 years earlier.

There are many different facets to the Sally story, some of which have been well aired in the press, and inevitably those that have not. Management and staff alike fought hard for the survival of the company and despite uninformed comment at the time, the truth is that the Finnish parent company deserves nothing but the utmost praise and respect for the way in which it continued to support the venture when others may well have walked away.

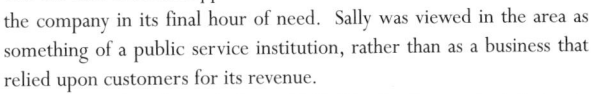

A personal sadness for me was the lack of local support for the company in its final hour of need. Sally was viewed in the area as something of a public service institution, rather than as a business that relied upon customers for its revenue.

In the final analysis, the loss of Sally Line is a loss to the industry in that it limits customer choice even further. Perhaps tellingly, we still receive calls from previously satisfied customers wishing to book crossings and who simply cannot believe that Sally is no more.

Bill Moses

Bill Moses
Sally UK Ltd, 1995-1998

The *Nuits Saint George* at Ramsgate during her 1980 season. *(Ferry Publications Library)*

In the early morning of 15th June 1981, *The Viking* commenced her inaugural sailing from Dunkerque to Ramsgate as the flagship of the newly created Sally Line. The ship arrived in a virtually unsheltered English port in the true traditions of her ancestors whose name she proudly displayed on her bows. The first season was a fairly short one and the early difficulties associated with the open aspect of the port gave an indication of some of the future problems that had to be overcome in order to maintain a regular ferry service with the minimum of disruption and cancellations.

The story of Sally Line is not only that of ships carrying passengers across the English Channel, but also the story of a ferry port. There are many ferry ports around the coast of the British Isles which are proud to boast the names of the well-known ferry operators who use their facilities but very few can claim that they owe their success, and possibly their very existence, to their main ferry user. In the annals of maritime history, the names of Ramsgate and Sally Line are synonymous.

The Kentish seaside resorts of Margate and Ramsgate have always been regular stage posts for pleasant seaside cruising, which gained in popularity after 1955 when 'No Passport' day excursions to France were introduced. The ships of the General Steam Navigation Company, the *Royal Daffodil* and the *Queen of the Channel* were well-known along the Kentish shores as well as in the French ports of Boulogne and Calais.

When the services ended in 1966, day-trippers migrated to the Dover-based ferry companies who received a boost in 1973 when Britain joined the Common Market and restrictions were lifted so that day-trippers could enjoy their duty free allowances without having to be out of Britain for at least twenty-four hours as was previously required.

An unsuccessful attempt to run a car ferry service between Ramsgate and Dunkerque West was made during the summer of 1980. Dunkerque - Ramsgate Ferries (DRF) encountered many problems and were finally forced to abandon the service amidst debts and the arrest of their ferry, the *Nuits St. Georges*.

The failure of DRF was viewed with some degree of sadness as a considerable amount of money had been invested in the provision of a linkspan and port facilities. The possibility of the port falling rapidly into decline was viewed with some consternation. Even so, there were many sceptics when it became known that another operator was interested in using the facilities of the port. This came about early in 1981 when it was announced by Thanet District Council that Rederi AB Sally was interested in reopening the Ramsgate -Dunkerque route. The company was willing to invest £5 million in the development of a new service and it was therefore recognized that the strong financial backing that was previously lacking was now available. In order to place the new company into perspective it would seem appropriate to give some idea of the size and success of the parent company in Finland.

Rederi AB Sally was at that time the largest privately owned shipping company in Finland. They started operations between Finland and Sweden in 1959 with the 1924-built, former British Railways steamer, *Dinard*, which, after a refit in Denmark, was named the *Viking* and put on the

Graddo-Mariehamn-Korppoo route under the Viking Line banner, remaining in service until 1970. Due to disagreements in the Viking Line, a breakaway group formed a rival company, Alandsfarjan AB and purchased another ex Southern Railway ship from Britain called the *Brittany* (built 1933), which was commissioned as the *Alandsfarjan* in 1963 and remained in service until 1972. By this time the original Viking Line had been renamed Rederi AB Sally and had made agreements with Alandsfarjan AB (renamed S-F Line) and Rederi AB Slite to form a marketing consortium known as Viking Line, with all vessels operating a common service under this banner.

1980

In 1980 Rederi AB Sally joined forces with Michael Kingshott, who had already assisted with the development of the new ferry facilities at Sheerness, to investigate the introduction of a new ferry service across the North Sea. At that time the company was looking for expansion abroad with Britain being the main target.

The short sea routes across the North Sea and the English Channel were already very busy and enormously competitive, but there appeared to be an obvious slot left by the demise of DRF the previous year and thus there was considerable potential to introduce a new service to meet the growing volume of traffic on the Channel. Mr Kingshott recognised that Thanet District Council had already invested approximately £6.25 million constructing a one-berth ferry facility and terminal at the West Rocks site at Ramsgate. If he could negotiate for these facilities there would be a golden opportunity for Rederi AB Sally to enter the cross-Channel market and develop a modern passenger and freight ro-ro port at a strategic location in the South-East where Dover, the traditional base for short-sea operations, was rapidly reaching saturation point. The fact that Thanet District Council had a ferry port without an operator gave Mr Kingshott a strong position from which to negotiate.

After various discussions with Thanet District Council Mr. Kingshott

The *Safe Christina* seen here in the English Channel in August 1981. (FotoFlite)

obtained, on behalf of Rederi AB Sally, a 90-year agreement to operate ferry services from Ramsgate, initially to Dunkerque.

1981

In April 1981, Rederi AB Sally made the final decision to launch the service with an investment of £5 million, to open a London office and to start on 15th June 1981. Mr Kingshott was appointed Managing Director of the new company, to be known as Sally Line Limited, and, despite the short time available in which to create an operating infrastructure and mount a marketing campaign, the service was launched on the due date, in time to capitalise on the peak summer traffic across the Channel.

The vessel for the new service was obtained from the parent company's fleet in Finland and the first ship chosen to operate on the route was the *Viking 5*, which had been in service across the Baltic Sea for about five years and was now considered to be too small for their needs due to expansion of services.

The *Viking 5* was built in 1974 by Jos. L Meyer of Papenburg in West Germany and was 5,286 gross tons with a capacity of 1,200 passengers, 220 cars/16 lorries and a service speed of 18.5 knots. Operations were marketed under the title of "Sally, the Viking Line", a small "Sally," monogram being added to the large white letters "Viking Line" on the vessel's red hull. An additional change to Baltic livery was the word "Sally," in a small yellow diamond on an otherwise red and white funnel, replacing the former black "V". Her crew was a mix of Finnish officers and deck crew with the catering and reception staff being French. For English Channel work the ship was renamed *The Viking*.

A twice daily service at 10.00 and 22.00 from Ramsgate with 07.00 and 19.00 from Dunkerque would be operated every day until 25th October. Services would then be suspended until the spring of 1982 when it was hoped to increase their frequency.

The ship first appeared in Ramsgate on 10th June but was unable to undertake actual berthing trials, as the linkspan had not yet been put back into place after being towed into the inner harbour on 24th October 1980 following the demise of DRF. A number of manoeuvres were executed, off the berth, to ensure that tug assistance would not be required, before *The Viking* then proceeded to the Thames where she was berthed alongside HMS *Belfast* for a courtesy visit. Travel trade and press guests were received on the following two days, 11th and 12th June before a leisurely overnight return to Ramsgate where she was able to berth successfully. An open day for the public was arranged for 13th June followed by further festivities next day with a visit to Dunkerque.

The first commercial sailing took place on the target day of 15th June with the 07.00 sailing from Dunkerque. The ship immediately settled into her routine, although there was initial reluctance on the part of the travelling public to use her. However, by July the 10.00 sailing regularly carried 600-700 passengers who took the opportunity of a two and a half hour trip each way for a day out in France. The company arranged for trippers to be conveyed to and from the city centre by coach, this being necessary due to Dunkerque West being somewhat wind-swept and also several miles from the town itself.

The ship quickly became very popular with her high standards of Scandinavian decor and service. Fares had been set at very competitive levels and catering facilities onboard had been maintained at Baltic standards with high quality food again at competitive prices. Lunch with a choice of Scandinavian hot or cold dishes was available at a cost of £4.80 while an á la carte selection was available in the restaurant at a cost of £3.60 to £5.90. All went well until 21st August when *The Viking* suffered a mechanical problem on passage from Dunkerque. After continuing on to Ramsgate to discharge passengers the ship limped back to Dunkerque on one engine for repairs. The service had to be suspended for three days while the company sought a replacement ship. The efficiency of the

The Viking arrives at Ramsgate from Dunkerque in October 1982. This view shows the port of Ramsgate prior to the breakwater being built for protection of the linkspan. *(John Hendy)*

company is demonstrated by the fact that a replacement was found within a few hours, the three days being required for the new ship to travel from the Baltic to Ramsgate and take on stores and fuel.

The replacement ship was the *Safe Christina*, built in 1969 as the *Prinsessan Christiana* for Goteborg-Frederikshavn Linjen of Sweden (trading as Sessan Linjen) for their service between Gothenburg and Frederikshavn. In 1979 she was sold to Consafe Offshore (an oil industry supply company) and chartered back to Sessan Linjen. The ship had a gross tonnage of 5,696 and with a capacity of 1,305 passengers and 250 cars, she was an ideal replacement for *The Viking*. For a route operating in daytime only and a crossing time of two and a half hours, a lower number of berths and greater lounge space made her that little more suitable for the service.

The *Safe Christina* re-opened the route on 24th August and remained in service until the close of the season on 25th October. During this period the open aspect of Ramsgate brought its share of problems for Sally Line in that the autumn gales created havoc with the schedules.

Due to operating difficulties at Ramsgate and 25% of scheduled sailings being lost, Sally Line entered into prolonged discussions throughout the winter months with Thanet District Council and these resulted in the reduction of £200,000 per annum from the port dues for a period of 20 years. The Council also agreed to dredge the channel approaches to the necessary minimum depth and provide a wide swinging area near to the harbour linkspan while Sally Line agreed to spend £1 million on a protective breakwater. The dredging was to start within a few weeks but, as the breakwater needed planning permission and as there were also some local objections, this was delayed until the outcome of a public enquiry.

In the meantime it was found that the damage to the engine of *The Viking* was much more severe than originally thought. The ship returned to Finland for more extensive work to be carried out and while deliberations were taking place she was used as a floating police barracks. It was not until the following year that the decision was taken to abandon the repair

The *Prinsessan Desiree* in the English Channel on her way to Ramsgate where she became the replacement ship for *Viking 6* in May 1982. (*FotoFlite*)

to the damaged engine. Instead, due to various problems, it was decided to replace both engines with new ones of more modern design. She was fitted with two new Deutz engines of 6,600 bhp each, replacing the original Smit Bolnes units of 5,500 bhp each. These repairs were finally completed in mid-May 1982.

1982

After completion of the dredging work in Ramsgate Harbour, the service recommenced on 1st May 1982. There was little time available to undertake the marketing effort necessary for what was effectively a total relaunch of the Sally Line operation. The company had to generate trade by offering fares considerably below those charged by other operators on the short sea routes and therefore was 'buying' much of its traffic. In addition, the earlier failure of DRF and Sally's own operating problems during the first season caused difficulties which resulted in a lack of support by the travel trade, for the service which only generated 30% of

The Viking at Ramsgate. *(Geoffrey Breeze collection)*

the company's UK bookings. These problems were overcome of course and the fact that 75% of Sally Line's bookings eventually came to be made by the travel trade demonstrates this.

The 1982 season was advertised as a two ship service and the second ship for this route was the much travelled *Viking 6*. The ship was built in 1967 by A/S Langesunds Mek. in Norway. Of 5,149 gross tons, she had passenger capacity for 1,200 and could carry 220 cars with a service speed of 22 knots. Her original owners were Stena Line, who named her the *Stena Britannica*. Unusually for a Baltic Sea ferry, the ship was fitted with Denny-Brown stabilisers (as was in fact the *Viking 5*). She was sold to the State of Alaska in 1968 and again sold, in 1974, this time to Rederi AB Sally of Finland, renamed the *Viking 6* and used on services across the Baltic Sea. She was chartered to Brittany Ferries in 1980 for services to St. Malo under the name *Goelo*, the charter terminating at the end of the 1981 summer season after which she returned to the Baltic and resumed the name *Viking 6*.

As *The Viking* was not quite ready to resume full service, it was decided to commence the season using the *Viking 6*. The new season was due to start on 1st May but unfortunately striking French dockers closed the port of Dunkerque and the service did not start until the following day. The troubles that had dogged Sally the previous year suddenly started to rear their heads again in that first month. Argentina invaded the Falkland Islands resulting in the declaration of war by Britain. The Ministry of Defence organised a Falkland Islands Task Force which included several merchant ships with some ro-ro car ferries among them, one of these ships being North Sea Ferries' the *Norland*. With a berth capacity of 454, North Sea Ferries became interested in the *Viking 6* and a charter was arranged as soon as she could be released by Sally Line. Fortunately it had already been decided to send *The Viking* back to Ramsgate and she arrived there on 20th May, resuming full service on the next day. The *Viking 6* sailed for Hull where she arrived on 22nd May. Although her stay at Ramsgate was rather short lived, as we shall see she eventually returned some years later under a different guise and flag and again became a firm favourite.

As the 1982 season had been advertised as a two ship service, it was necessary to find another ship. Luckily, it was discovered that the *Prinsessan Desiree* was available for charter, this ship being an identical sister to the *Safe Christina*, the ship chartered for the previous season. As she had proved to be very suitable, there were no qualms about introducing her sister on the route. When she arrived in Ramsgate on 25th June she was still in her Sessan Linjen livery of white hull and she retained her own name on the bow although she bore the legend "Sally Viking 2" painted on the hull together with a Sally monogram on her funnel. She remained with this scheme throughout her season at Ramsgate.

Passenger and vehicle loadings quickly built up and by the end of July it was a common sight for both morning departures from Ramsgate to take over 800 passengers and a full complement of cars. By offering sensible and competitive fares without complications and an extensive advertising campaign, Sally the Viking Line seemed to be succeeding in winning traffic from other ferry operators along the English Channel. Following the successful summer season, *The Viking* returned to Germany early in September for an overhaul and tuning of her new engines, before returning to Ramsgate by the middle of September to operate a winter service for the first time. During the overhaul, the *Prinsessan Desiree* maintained the advertised autumn single ship service after which her charter ended.

As well as the problem of the departure of the *Viking 6* for the North Sea, the company's sailings were again disrupted that year due to operating from the exposed berth which had no protection from adverse winds and tidal conditions. In view of these circumstances the company looked at the possibility of using Dover as an alternative to Ramsgate and also examined the viability of running into Dunkerque East. The lock system there would have caused operational problems.

A further complication was that the parent company, Rederi AB Sally, made a number of vessel changes at short notice in order to redeploy the vessels to other services and operations within their group.

1983

Adverse weather conditions were affecting the port of Ramsgate and the company announced that if work did not start soon on the proposed breakwater they would look elsewhere for a terminal, as they were no longer prepared to accept public criticism. Early in the season, as compensation for the dredging costs of £1 million spent by Thanet District Council, a 25% reduction from car bookings and 10% from passenger bookings was arranged for local residents. As winter services were in operation for the first time, some attractive offers of £4 day returns were made which went a long way to filling some of the empty seats on sailings made primarily for cargo traffic to the Continent.

The high level of lost sailings at Ramsgate resulted in Rederi AB Sally

The German-built *Njegos* was only to have a short spell on the Ramsgate-Dunkerque service in 1984. The vessel later became the *Tregestel* for Brittany Ferries. She currently operates for P&O Scottish Ferries as the *St. Clair*. (FotoFlite)

agreeing to Michael Kingshott's proposal to undertake extensive research to establish the optimum way of protecting the harbour. By the time work was able to start on the breakwater the cost had risen to £2.5 million. A model of the tidal and wind conditions at Ramsgate Harbour was constructed at the Technical Research Centre at Helsinki University and tank tests were carried out on a scheme to construct a further breakwater which would enclose an area where it was proposed to build three additional linkspans (together with parking facilities and cargo areas), the whole area having a minimum depth of 6.5 metres at low tide. A scheme for a protective breakwater was devised from this research to be implemented in three stages: -

1983: An arm of the breakwater be built from the existing land area
1984: Two island breakwaters to be constructed.
1985/6: A full wrap-round breakwater to be completed.

In view of the considerable expenditure which was necessary to

The *Viking 3* is seen here outward bound from Ramsgate to Dunkerque in April 1983. (FotoFlite)

provide the port protection, a decision was taken in 1983 to explore the possibility of developing Ramsgate as a port for other operators, thus reducing the financial burden on Sally Line Limited. As a result the UK company was reorganised in 1983 into a holding company, Sally UK Holdings PLC, with two operating subsidiaries, Sally Line Limited, to operate the ferry services, and Port Ramsgate Limited, to develop and operate the port. The two operating companies followed a policy of separate development.

The parent company in Finland inflicted a further change of ship in April 1983. The new vessel was the *Viking 3*, which entered service at Ramsgate on 12th April. The change was probably not noticed by the travelling public as the *Viking 3* was in fact another sister ship of *The Viking* (ex *Viking 5*), built by J. L Meyer. Having been built for Baltic Sea services in 1972, the ship had been sold out of service in 1976 to Vaasanlaivat Oy of Finland for services across the Gulf of Bothnia In October 1982, her owners were taken over by Rederi AB Sally and thus the ship which had been renamed the *Wasa Express* came back to her previous owners. As *The Viking* was a lengthened version of the sister ships with a greater number of berths than the *Wasa Express*, it was decided to swap the ships round to take advantage of the increased number of berths on the longer route in Finland. Ramsgate gained some benefit due to the increase in lounge area of the *Wasa Express* which reverted to her original name of the *Viking 3*. *The Viking*, after returning to Finland, was given a new livery and renamed the *Sally Express*. She was sold again in March 1984 to Fred Olsen Line of Norway and renamed the *Bollete*.

A two ship service was planned to run from 8th July and the company acquired the Danish ferry *Kalle III* of 4,371 gross tons from Jydsk Faergefart. The ship had been built at Bremerhaven in 1974 as the *Kattegatt II* and introduced into service between Juelsminde (Jutland) and Kalundborg (Sealand) as the *Kalle III*, her original name never being used.

Having had their fair share of problems with ships being re-allocated by the parent company in Finland, Sally took the *Kalle III* on a long term bareboat charter with an option to purchase. A £3 million refit was carried out by her builders AG Weser of Bremerhaven to make her suitable for Channel operations. These included the fitting of stabilisers, a large duty-free shop and, an unusual feature, an escalator to carry passengers from the car deck to the public lounge area.

It was intended that the new ship, which was renamed *The Viking*, would enter service on 8th July, but there were teething problems and she did not arrive until 17th July when she made her inaugural sailing. At this time she retained her Danish registry and ran with her Danish crew. The Danish crew remained with the ship until the end of the season when she went for a further refit which included an extension to her already large duty free shop. While this was taking place she was reflagged, registered in Mariehamn and was taken over by a Finnish crew for the first time.

In October 1983, after an agreement between Port Ramsgate and Charles Schiaffino, a new cargo service commenced from Ramsgate to Ostend with one trip daily by Schiaffino Line. This French company already ran a twice daily service from Dover to Ostend but, due to the

The Viking arrives off Dunkerque in June 1981. *(FotoFlite)*

An impressive view of the *Viking 6*. (Mike Louagie)

pending closure of her Dover berth, were known to be looking for another port. On 4th October their *Schiaffino*, built in 1970 and with a capacity for 36 trailers, switched from Dover to Ramsgate, using Ramsgate's single linkspan when it was not occupied by a Sally Line vessel. Michael Kingshott stated that the arrival of a second operator would enable development plans to proceed at a greater pace than previously expected. A second berth was completed in February 1984 and Schiaffino moved its entire operation from Dover to Ramsgate, thus bringing two further ships to the expanding port. These were the *Catherine Schiaffino*, built in 1978 with a capacity of 50 trailers, and the *Rose Schiaffino*, built in 1972 also with a 50 trailer capacity.

1984

A sign of things going well at Ramsgate was the need to keep the *Viking 3* in a freight role at the end of the 1983 season instead of the ship being returned to the Baltic as originally planned. From October, the *Viking 3* made six overnight round trips per week, taking up to a maximum of 27 trailers. She continued in this role until March 1984 when she returned to the Baltic and resumed her name as the *Wasa Express*, remaining in service as such until 1988 when she was sold to Eckero Line and renamed the *Roslagen*.

With the completion of the first phase of Port Ramsgate's development (the construction of the second berth together with the reclamation of 25,000 square metres of land), thoughts turned quickly to the second phase - the long awaited provision of two breakwaters with a total length of 430 metres about 500 metres offshore. Port Ramsgate awarded the £1.25 million contract to John Howard & Company PLC in July 1984 for the construction of the breakwaters and further land reclamation with work commencing immediately. The entire operation was marine-based so that minimum disruption would occur in the port itself. It had already been calculated that the amount of rock needed would be 80,000 tons with a breakwater height of 9 metres.

The work was completed by November 1984, and although the two breakwaters were not connected together at this stage, there was much improvement in protection of the harbour from the wave height that previously caused problems.

The 1984 service was promoted to a two ship operation from 2nd July until 29th September and it was thought that the *Viking 3* would revert to a passenger role for the summer, but as we have seen she was returned to Finland in March and was no longer available, the old problem of re-allocation of ships by the parent company having reared its head again. Sally Line had partially solved this problem by chartering (through the Finnish parent company) their new *The Viking* for all year round service but there was still a problem over the second ship for summer service only. It was announced in April that a newly chartered ship would be made available and this turned out to be a rather interesting choice in that she was an almost identical sister to *The Viking* (ex *Kalle III*) having been built at the same yard in Bremerhaven. The ship was the Yugoslavian registered *Njegos* of 3,999 gross tons. She was built in 1971 as the *Travemunde* for GT

Ruten, for their Gedser and Travemunde route and was sold for service between Yugoslavia, Italy and Greece following the completion of the new *Travemunde* in 1981. The ship, which had identical M.A.N. engines to *The Viking*, was repainted in the red and white livery of Sally Line but retained her name, port of registry and many of her Yugoslavian crew (although the catering staff were French). Prior to joining the Sally fleet the ship had been briefly chartered by Brittany Ferries.

During the winter and spring of 1984 *The Viking* made two sailings each day and these were supplemented in the summer with the acquisition of the *Njegos* so that four sailings were made each day to Dunkerque. Freight traffic also built up considerably and this put Sally Line on target for capturing 10% of the share of short-sea passenger, vehicle and freight traffic by 1985. Despite hints that Sally were intending to retain a two ship service until the end of the year, these plans were laid to rest when it was learned that Brittany Ferries, who having previously chartered the *Niegos* in the spring, now wished to acquire the ship on a more permanent basis. Sally Line released the ship at the end of September, thus ending any thought that the company may have had of running two identical ships, with obvious advantages. In any event, the *Niegos* was transferred to the Brittany Ferries fleet for service between Plymouth and Roscoff as the *Tregastel*.

Passenger figures for 1984 were quite impressive showing that the company had exceeded 600,000 passengers and 85,000 cars, and with aims to increase these figures the following year the company set higher targets and continued to strive for a 10% share of the cross Channel market.

With the *Niegos* no longer available, Sally Line were back almost to square one with their usual problem of short-lived ships, albeit not their main ship, and began the process of looking for another vessel to support what was planned to be a two ship service from April 1985 with up to five sailings per day. But before the *Niegos* left for Brittany Ferries, *The Viking* was sent for an early overhaul with the company breaking new ground by sending her to a British yard for the first time. They even supported a yard

A stern view of the well appointed *Viking 6* whilst on charter to Sally Line in 1985. *(FotoFlite)*

After her refit in Bremerhaven, the *Kalle III* emerged as Sally's new *The Viking* as seen in this picture crossing the English Channel on her way to Dunkerque. *(FotoFlite)*

The *Viking 3* approaches Ramsgate in April 1983. *(FotoFlite)*

in their home county when the ship was sent to Thames Ship Repairers at Chatham, thus providing jobs for the local Kent workforce.

Cargo traffic carried by Sally Line had built up considerably and the company was known to be interested in obtaining a cargo-only vessel. In the event, an agreement was reached with the French company, Compagnie General Maritime, for a joint service to commence on 20th November using the French company's ship the *Le Mans*, 4,153 gross tons (built in 1978) and capable of carrying 74 freight units. The new company called Sally/CGM Freight Service operated one service per day, Sundays to Fridays. The joint venture was looked upon as a major advance in establishing Ramsgate as a key Channel gateway.

With the completion of the two breakwaters, the reliability of service was assured from November 1984, but the expansion of the port was to continue much more. It was clear that a third linkspan would be needed and in early 1985 a further contract was signed with John Howard & Co for further land reclamation, strengthening and widening of the existing breakwater. Work would include joining of the two sections plus the construction of an extra section of breakwater from the end of the eastern arm of the Royal Harbour and extending in a south-easterly direction, thus narrowing the port entrance. This phase of the development would cost £5 million. The third linkspan itself was supplied by the Mattsson Group of Sweden at a cost of £700,000 and was ready for use in May 1985.

1985

Early in 1985 the company dropped the words 'the Viking' from its trading name. Previously marketed as 'Sally the Viking Line' it became simply 'Sally Line'. The company also announced that from April of that year they would be introducing a second ship and would be operating up to five return sailings a day on the route with some of the lowest fares on the Channel.

By February of 1985 it was clear from advance bookings that the company would enjoy a 40% increase in passenger and vehicle traffic. It appeared that although their television advertising campaign had not yet started, many holidaymakers were worried about consolidation of air tours and possible surcharges and were switching in droves to surface travel and taking their cars with them to the Continent. The five return sailings a day in the peak summer months would easily cope with these figures.

For the 1985 season Sally Line brought back a former vessel to join *The Viking* at Ramsgate from April. The ship was the *Viking 6* and readers will remember that this ship served the route for a short time in 1982 before transferring to Hull for service with North Sea Ferries. Since that time the ship had been sold to Sol Maritime Services of Cyprus, renamed the *Sol Olympia* and used on their service between Venice and Haifa. The ship was chartered back to Rederi AB Sally in early 1985 for service in the Baltic. As she was renamed the *Sun Express* it was expected that she would enter service with Sally subsidiary Vaassanlaivat, whose ships generally include the word 'Express' in their name. However this was not so, and she was introduced at Ramsgate after refurbishment at Thames Ship Repairers at Chatham. After her refit, the ship was capable of carrying 1,000 passengers, 220 cars, coaches and freight.

From 1st April four sailings were offered in each direction, but during peak summer months a fifth crossing was inserted into the timetable.

The ship retained the name *Sun Express* for about two months, after which she was again renamed the *Viking 6* but retained her Cypriot registry throughout her period with Sally Line which lasted for 12 months. During this period it became fairly obvious that the ship was not as compatible with *The Viking* as the company would have wished. Although she was a firm favourite with the travelling public, with her excellent accommodation which included lavish amounts of wood panelling in her companionways and public rooms and her kindly sea behaviour, she had a large amount of cabin accommodation which the company found difficult to utilise on the comparatively short sea crossings with no overnight sailings. The car deck also lacked height, which made her unsuitable for the larger freight vehicles that were being used in increasing numbers. Towards the end of the year, the company began looking for another ship.

In July 1985, Sally Line carried their two millionth passenger. More than 250,000 passengers used the route during the first five months of 1985 which was an increase of 57.8% over the corresponding period for 1984. Increases in vehicle traffic were also noted: coach traffic by 58%, car traffic by 42% and trailers and caravans by 63%.

1986

Passenger and freight capacity was increased by about 25% from April 1986 when Sally introduced a larger ferry to replace the *Viking 6*. As stated earlier, this ship had been considered an incompatible running mate for *The Viking* and during 1985 Sally had to turn away business because the *Viking 6* was really too small for the route. The new ship was the 5,300 gross tons *Gedser* which was bareboat chartered for a period of five years from GT Ruten of Denmark who had employed the vessel exclusively on the Gedser-Travemunde service.

Sally spent £1 million in converting and refitting the ship for their own needs, the refit almost becoming a total internal rebuild, at the Bremer Vulkan-Rickmers Werft shipyard at Bremerhaven, before she entered service on 25th April 1986. The ship was the first on the route with internal ramps to both vehicle decks which would ensure fast loading and unloading. Her car decks were able to carry 350 cars or 50 x 15 metre lorries, compared with 170 cars or 16 freight vehicles on the *Viking 6*. Her passengers capacity of 1,400 was reduced for the Sally service to 1,250 compared to the 800 of the *Viking 6*.

The refit provided the ship with a 230 square metre duty-free supermarket with four check-outs: a main restaurant with carvery/smorgasbord with a seating capacity of 335, a cafeteria for 450, two bars, a pub, perfume and gift shop, children's playroom, nursery and casino area.

Renamed the *Viking 2* the ship became the seventh ship to serve Sally

An aerial view of the port of Dunkerque West, showing the new Sally Line terminal with *The Viking* at the linkspan. An impressive covered walkway took passengers from the ship to the terminal. To the south of the Sally complex was the SNCF train ferry terminal. *(John Hendy collection)*

Line in their six years on the Ramsgate - Dunkerque service and the company was convinced that they had now found a permanent running mate for *The Viking*. One of the many problems faced by Sally in previous years was the lack of permanent vessels on the route with constant changes being made by the Finnish parent company. The problem was partially solved with the introduction of *The Viking* as a permanent ship but until now the second ship had been the subject of many changes. The *Viking 2* entered service on Friday 25th April flying the flag of the Bahamas. She sailed with a complete French crew from the Captain, officers, deck and catering crew to reception staff. Sally Line again offered four sailings per day increasing

This publicity shot for Sally Line shows The Viking *and the* Viking 2 *manoeuvring off the berth at Ramsgate. (Ferry Publications Library)*

to five per day during the summer season which ended on 12th September.

In Dunkerque, the Port Authority spent Fr8 million on a new side loading facility, completed in June, that gave direct access to the *Viking 2's* upper car deck, enabling the ship to unload cars and lorries from both decks at the same time.

A new luxury terminal for the exclusive use of Sally Line passengers was planned for completion in 1987. The terminal which initially included one new berth was located close to the SNCF rail ferry berth at Port Ouest. Built by the Port Autonome de Dunkerque, the terminal at the Quai de Ramsgate was the first of its kind and the most advanced in Europe and would enable passengers to walk direct to or from the ship through enclosed 'skywalks' in comfort whatever the weather conditions. It had been designed jointly by Sally and the Port Autonome de Dunkerque. Features included underground parking areas for coaches and cars, escalators to the passenger skywalk, a cafeteria, children's playroom, nursery, bureau de change and a full range of support facilities. Conference facilities for up to 300 delegates were also provided in what Sally's Managing Director called 'the new super city at Port Ouest'.

The linkspans were similar to the two double-width ones that Sally had built as part of its Ramsgate development scheme. Michael Kingshott announced that the new terminal had been designed to be enlarged so as to meet the future growth needs of Sally. "The investment in the new terminal, and the decision to go ahead with it after the signing of the Channel Tunnel agreement, amply demonstrates Dunkerque's confidence in the long term future of Sally Line," said Mr Kingshott. "It is being financed at a cost of £6 million by the port authority, which is also building a new sideloading linkspan for coaches and cars at Sally's terminal in Dunkerque. Our French colleagues recognise the long term future of Sally Line, with or without the Channel Tunnel. The confidence they have displayed in investing in this new terminal should be a salutary lesson to the moaning minnies in Britain who claim that a fixed link will mean ruin for the ferry operators."

"We are budgeting on a 25% increase in traffic during 1986 following the introduction of the *Viking 2* on the route and with an enormous upswing predicted in the number of people taking their cars abroad, I see no reason why that sort of growth should not continue in the years ahead," said Mr. Kingshott. The contract for the new terminal was signed on-board *The Viking* on 25th March with work on the new terminal planned to begin three months later. The first stage of the new terminal was to cover around 25 acres with a further 60 acres available for future development.

Summer 1986 saw the long-awaited completion of the new Ramsgate breakwater in which the two isolated sections were joined together and a second breakwater built from the eastern arm of the Royal Harbour to narrow the harbour entrance. Reclamation of land had also taken place to provide 26,000 square metres of hard-standing for a car park, freight marshalling yards and other much needed facilities. This brought the total cost of spending on the port to date to £14 million. Land was reclaimed by the importation of 'infill' from the nearby Goodwin Sands and by reducing and utilising the material from some high spots in the approaches to the port entrance channel.

With the completion of the breakwaters, plans were made for further development and the spending of a further £3 million to provide the port with all the facilities a modern freight and passenger port required to survive the competitive climate of the 1990's. Negotiations took place again with Thanet District Council resulting in Sally extending the lease on the port to 125 years.

The introduction of the *Viking 2* with her greater carrying capacity, produced major inroads into the short sea route cross-Channel market. July figures showed an increase of 29% in coach carrying over the previous year. Indeed, over the first seven months of the year, coach traffic had increased by 41% over the corresponding period of 1985. Passenger and car traffic was also running at record levels with increases being quoted over the corresponding period of 1985 as 28% and 14% respectively showing that Sally Line were well on the way to achieving their aim of a 25% increase on all traffic following the introduction of the *Viking 2*. Sally celebrated the carrying of their three millionth passenger with a champagne reception on board the *Viking 2*.

During 1987 there was a reorganisation of Sally Line's parent company in Finland but it had very little effect on the services of the British company. In February of that year the majority holding in Rederi AB Sally (in Finland) was transferred from the Union Bank of Finland to Oy Efljohn-Trading AB, the principal owners being EffoaFinland Steamship Co. of Helsinki and Johnson Line AB of Stockholm. The new company name was changed to Rederi AB Effjohn, this being the new parent company of Rederi AB Sally.

The outcome of these proceedings was that in October 1987 Rederi AB Sally sold its 33% share of the Viking Line, while the other two partners in Viking Line bought up an equally large part of Sally's shareholding.

Mid-July saw the opening of Sally's new terminal at Dunkerque. The two ships, *The Viking* and the *Viking 2* switched from the original berth used since 1980, when the service from Ramsgate was inaugurated by DRF. As before, both ships unloaded bow-in at the new double width linkspan similar to those already installed at Ramsgate. The pattern of sailings was similar to the previous year with four return trips per day increasing to five from 10th July to 13th September. The sailing times were: from Ramsgate at 09.00, 11.30, 16.00, 19.30, 23.00 and from Dunkerque at 08.30, 13.30, 17.00, 20.30 and 23.59.

Sally Line achieved another record breaking year on its Ramsgate-Dunkerque route in 1987, despite little real growth in the cross-Channel market in general. Passenger figures were up by 3% to 1,243,536; car and caravan traffic was more than 2% up to 134,920 vehicles; while freight

The newly-arrived *Viking 2* swings off the berth at Ramsgate prior to entering service. *(Ferry Publications Library)*

traffic jumped a massive 24% to 47,537 units. Although Sally Line were in the throes of changing their public image, the increase in business during the year indicated that the company was providing exactly what the market place required.

1988

Sally Line continued to make the most of these figures and used them to advantage when planning their 1988 brochure. The number of sailings per day was increased from four to five all year round from 24th March instead of summer peak periods only.

Both ships went for their annual refit which included up-grading and refurbishment at the start of the year, going in turn this time to Southampton with *The Viking* being out of service in January and the *Viking 2* in early February. A reduced single ship service operated until both ships returned to duty on 10th February.

During the early part of 1988 the British seamen's unions commissioned one of their regular strikes, this one being primarily concerned with reduced manning levels planned for implementation by P & O European Ferries on their Dover - Calais service which brought the ships to a standstill. Crews from other operators came out in sympathy so that no British crewed ships sailed out of Dover. Sally Line was not affected by the dispute and their ships sailed normally and benefited from Dover's loss, resulting in a staggering increase in all areas of Sally Line's business through the port of Ramsgate. The two ship service carried 592,203 passengers in the five months to the end of April, a 49% increase on the same period for the previous year, while car and caravan traffic was up by 78% to 61,236 vehicles. The number of coaches also increased by 63% to 7,130. There was also a significant increase in the number of advance bookings for the period June - September, this being up by 49.5% on a similar period for 1987. Sally Line management recognised these figures as a demonstration of faith by their customers in Sally Line's reliability and high standards. It seemed that indeed 'Sally Line had got it right across the

Above: The *Sally Star* outward bound from Ramsgate. *(FotoFlite)*

An outstanding aerial view of the Ramsgate terminal with two Sally Line vessels *The Viking* and *Sally Star* and the freight ship *Catherine Schiaffino*. *(FotoFlite)*

Channel' at last after much effort and hard work on their part to overcome the problems experienced during the early years of the service from Ramsgate.

Sally Line demonstrated great faith in their own future when they announced in May 1988 that they would be introducing their own 'Jumbo' ferry on the route at the end of the year as a replacement for the faithful *The Viking*. The new ship was the 9,210 gross tons *Travemunde Link* which at that time was running for GT-Link from Travemunde in Germany to the Danish port of Gedser. The ship had a length of 137.4 metres with a breadth of 22.3 metres. Her carrying capacity was 450 cars, 64 x 15-metre lorries and 1,800 passengers. By coincidence the new ship would be running with an old partner in that both she and the *Viking 2* as the *Gedser*, served together on the Travemunde - Gedser route, until Sally Line chartered her for a five year period in 1985. The new ship, built by Wartsila of Helsinki in 1981, was chartered by Sally Line for a period of five years and was expected to he given a 'Viking' name when introduced into service on the route. The ship demonstrated the company's long term commitment and determination to take on the challenge of the Channel Tunnel. After a refit at Tilbury, the *Travemunde Link* boasted two restaurants, a cafeteria, three bars and a wide range of other on-board facilities and leisure areas, the whole refit (including the installation of additional safety equipment for English Channel operations and new English and French directional signs throughout the passenger areas) costing in the region of £650,000. Sally Line Chairman, Michael Kingshott said, "The introduction of this much bigger vessel is another reflection of the growing demand for Sally Line. Our only regret is that it will mean more traffic through the streets of Ramsgate. I hope that the opponents of Kent County Council's harbour access road applications will ponder on the inconvenience their opposition to the plan will cause to their fellow townsfolk."

Despite disappointment which followed the Minister's refusal of the Kent County Council harbour road plan, the Sally Group had no plans to cut back on its commitment to Thanet. The Group had by this time invested £17 million in developing Ramsgate - now Kent's second busiest port - into one of the most modern and efficient ports in Britain. August saw the opening of a new double width linkspan which would be the permanent berth for Sally Line ships. This together with other associated works cost £750,000 and replaced the previous single linkspan which had been in use since 1981.

The linkspans then numbered three - Schiaffino using the second, while the third was used mainly for ships bringing import cars into Britain, business which Port Ramsgate has been remarkably successful in attracting. More than 26,000 trade cars were handled through Port Ramsgate in the first seven months of 1988.

While the new ferry was at Tilbury undergoing her refit, there was considerable activity behind the scenes. Following the take-over of Rederi AB Sally in 1987 and the severing of Viking Line connections in October 1987, plus the change in company image at Sally Line, several thoughts had been given concerning the naming of the ships and company livery. The previous livery of red hull and white superstructure was thought to be rather aggressive and so as part of the new image it was decided to cut down on the amount of red in the livery and use more white in common with many other ferry operators. Therefore instead of the whole of the ships' hulls being painted red, only the lower half would be this colour with the remainder being white. The funnel colour would also be simplified in that it would be white with two slim red bands near the top. The word 'Sally' would be painted on the white section of the hull in red letters. The major change as far as the ships were concerned was that the new arrival would enter service without a 'Viking' name and would be the first permanent ship in the company's history to do so - even the *Prinsessan Desiree* had *Viking 2* painted on her hull while acting as a summer relief ship. The name chosen was the *Sally Star* and it was announced that the *Viking 2* would he renamed the *Sally Sky* after her refit in December.

The *Sally Star* entered service on 6th December and hit the pre-Christmas headlines of the national press on 20th December. The vessel was half an hour out of Ramsgate and about two and a half miles off-shore with

The *Sally Sky* at Zeebrugge on 23rd November 1989. The ship had been diverted due to industrial action in France. *(Mike Louagie)*

373 passengers on board when a fire broke out in the engine room. The crew immediately sealed it off and alerted the fire services with 25 Kent firemen being airlifted by helicopters from RAF Manston just outside Ramsgate, while several ships and a lifeboat stood by. The passengers were evacuated to the upper decks where they remained calm and were fed by the ship's crew. *The Viking* initially tried to take the ship in tow but this was unsuccessful and the *Sally Star* eventually arrived in Ramsgate under tow by tug. The passengers spoke very highly of the officers and crew during the emergency, praising the Captain for his calming influence and the continual information that he gave to them, revising and updating every 15 minutes.

In order to maintain schedules throughout the busy pre-Christmas period, the *Viking 2* had to be summoned from her refit by ARNO in Dunkerque (where she was also to be renamed the *Sally Sky*) to join *The Viking*. Both vessels continued to operate together until 7th January 1989 when the *Botnia Express* arrived from Finland to take over from *The Viking* which had a pre-arranged charter to cover the B & I Line service between Holyhead and Dublin while their normal ship was away for overhaul.

1989

While the *Sally Star* was undergoing repairs, the thoughts of Sally's managers were still on future growth and a study was made into the possibility of 'jumboizing' the ship by extending her 30 metres and adding additional accommodation. The overall cost of the project was estimated at £10 million with the ship being in the yard for two months in order to complete the work, an additional three to four months being required prior to this for preparations to be made. In the event Sally abandoned this particular project.

The *Sally Star* left the repair yard on the morning of 26th January for sea trials and trial berthing at Dover Eastern Docks to confirm that the ship would be able to dock there in an emergency although Sally officials emphasised that the company had no plans to switch from Ramsgate to Dover. Following her visit to Dover the ship returned to Dunkerque in the evening in order to take up the 08.30 sailing on the following morning after which the *Botnia Express* returned to Finland.

Apart from foul weather conditions in February 1989 which prevented many other operators from sailing or docking on time, the *Sally Star* had no further problems and together with the *Sally Sky* provided an good standard of service across the English Channel.

The Sally Group had an interesting view of the Channel Tunnel project and had no worries at the time in 1989 about its effect on their future. Sally viewed the tunnel project as a balance between transport and leisure. The aim of Sally on the arrival of the tunnel was to offer a happy medium. Travelling through the tunnel on the rail link, they felt would be restrictive. Hovercraft travel across the Channel would be the same. On the other hand crossing the Channel by ferry instead of through the tunnel would be a leisure experience, the degree of which would depend on the facilities offered by the ferry operators. A further consideration was that passengers wanted to travel from A to B in a reasonably short time. If they chose the leisurely ferry route the speed of the crossing must allow them the opportunity to enjoy the experience. With a two and a half hour crossing time, the Ramsgate -Dunkerque route offered the best balance between leisure and travel.

The *Sally Sky*, as built, was somewhat 'packed to the gunnels' and in order to redress the imbalance with the flagship *Sally Star*; in terms of freight capacity, and also to prepare her for 1992, she underwent a major refit in January 1990 at which time she was literally cut in two and her length increased by 20.8 metres with the fitting of a new centre section. The ship was divided so that the engine room and machinery spaces were not affected in any way. Her capacity was increased by about thirty extra cars and an additional ten 15 metre freight/trailer units.

As well as the extra freight capacity, the refit included total refurbishment making full use of the increase in the length of the vessel. Additional facilities included: a totally new concept in fast food operation to replace the cafeteria, a new reception area, improved seating for passengers.

When *The Viking* went off on charter to the Irish Sea in January 1989, the *Botnia Express* was summoned from the Baltic Sea to cover the service. The vessel is seen here whilst on charter to Sally Line. *(FotoFlite)*

The refit of both ships was carried out at the Immingham-based Humber Ship Repairers Ltd. The *Sally Star* was the first ship to be improved and left Ramsgate on 27th December 1989 for her 16 day refit returning to Ramsgate in time for Sally Sky to leave on 19th January 1990 for a somewhat longer period of almost three months.

Whilst the refit of both vessels took place, regular travellers were able to renew their acquaintance with the faithful *The Viking* currently running across the Gulf of Bothnia in Vaasanlaivat livery as the *Wasa Prince*.

1990

For the 1990 season both the *Sally Sky* and *Sally Star* appeared in the company's new livery. Both ships also had their passengers certificates reduced, the *Sally Sky*'s became 1,500 (previously 1,800) while the *Sally Star*'s was reduced to 1,050 (previously 1,150).

Following the company's abortive bid to acquire Isle of Wight operators Red Funnel in 1989, Sally Line acquired the Ramsgate-based ro-

The *Wasa Prince* (ex *The Viking*) pictured during January 1990 whilst on passage to Ramsgate. *(FotoFlite)*

link. On 15th June, Sally Ferries celebrated their tenth birthday with a special crossing of the *Sally Sky* on her 09.00 sailing from Ramsgate to France.

On the freight side, in order to boost the the unaccompanied freight on the new Ostend link, Sally took the Romanian-owned *Bazias 3* and *Bazias 4* on charter. Each boasted a capacity for 50 x 12 metre trailers and accommodation for twelve drivers. Extra berths were not essential as excess drivers could then reach Ostend via Dover.

Over the next couple of years, with fierce competition on the Dover Strait, Sally Line continued their regular sailings but with a gradual reduction in passenger numbers with improved services from Dover and later with the opening of the Channel Tunnel, the company were forced to reduce their fares in order to compete.

ro ferry operator Charles Schiaffino and at last gained a second route and access to a Belgian port.

At the end of the summer season, a further bout of strikes by dockers at Dunkerque saw Sally Line services suspended between 30th September and 30th October. Problems occurred when the Port Authority tried to introduce similar working patterns to those over the border in Belgium. During this industrial dispute, the company were only able to operate a freight-only service between Ramsgate and Zeebrugge.

1991

Both Sally Line vessels refitted at Dunkerque and during the period of overhaul again brought in the *Wasa Prince* (ex *The Viking*) to maintain the

The much-travelled *Nord Neptunus* (ex *Darnia*) is seen here whilst on charter to Sally Line. *(FotoFlite)*

The British-crewed *Sally Sky* at full speed. A side loading door can be seen on her portside. *(FotoFlite)*

This interesting view shows the train ferry *Nord Pas-de-Calais* and the Sally freight vessel *Sally Sun* at Dunkerque Ouest. *(John Bryant)*

1992

The charter of the *Nord Neptunus* (ex Sealink's *Darnia*) occurred early in the year to cover the overhaul periods. She had been built as the *Stena Topper* in 1976 and had been resold to Swedish owners Nordstrom & Thulin in the previous year.

1993

On 22nd September, the Belgian Government announced that they planned to move their Ostend service from Dover in favour of Ramsgate. Their decision brought 147 years of history to an end but it offered a major boost not only to the Port of Ramsgate but also to Sally Line's operations. The new agreement between Regie voor Maritiem Transport (RMT who traded as Oostende Lines) and Sally was based on a five year, 50-50 partnership and the route between Ramsgate and Ostend would commence as from 1st January 1994. As part of the agreement, Sally Line's freight service to Ostend would continue but it was agreed by both partners that at least £6 million worth of modifications would be undertaken at Ramsgate to expand both RMT and Sally Line's freight operations. Among the improvements at the Kentish port was the provision of a new linkspan and the charter of two tugs. The biggest headache for Ramsgate would be the 28,833 gross ton superferry *Prins Filip* and there were those that believed that this huge vessel would be too large for the port. In readiness for her arrival both the approach channel and the swinging area off the berth required further dredging.

The port infrastructure and level of facilities at Ramsgate were at the time badly in need of modernisation and represented a sharp contrast to those experienced elsewhere along the English Channel. The approach road through the old town was far too confined and was for the next six years to be an aggravating factor for all operations. One of the reasons for Sally Line's enthusiasm to add the Belgian operation to the port was that it would allow them to purchase RMT when it was privatised and they also hoped that the increased traffic generated by the new company might persuade Kent County Council to build the new access road to their port.

During October, Sally Line's chartered Romanian freighters were

The recently repainted *Schiaffino* in Sally livery leaves Ostend on a special press trip in 1993. *(Mike Louagie)*

renamed. The *Bazias 3* became the *Sally Euroroute*, while the *Bazias 4* became the *Sally Eurolink*. Both vessels were re-registered in Nassau following their renaming.

Prior to the end of the year, RMT's vessels undertook berthing trials at Ramsgate. First was the *Reine Astrid* followed by the *Princesse Marie-Christine* and then, on 31st December, the *Prins Albert*. The berthing trials proved to be very unsatisfactory and there were concerns expressed by senior RMT officers that the service was not really ready to commence as from 1st January 1994.

1994

In spite of the earlier problems, the new RMT (trading as Oostende Lines) operation commenced as from 1st January but without the flagship *Prins Filip*, as the dredging had not been completed at the Kentish port, and without the fast ferry operation of the Boeing Jetfoils.

The *Prins Filip* did eventually take up service and undertook the long-awaited trials at Ramsgate on 27th January. The weather conditions were

The *Sally Sky* and *Sally Star* pass each other in mid-Channel whilst operating on the Ramsgate-Dunkerque service. *(FotoFlite)*

The Manx-registered freighter *Gute* seen outward bound from Ramsgate in Sally livery whilst on charter to the company. The vessel later became the *Sally Sun*. *(FotoFlite)*

not at all favourable at the time, with strong WSW winds blowing between 30 and 45 knots. She duly arrived off the Kentish port but due to a tragic accident involving a quartermaster on the *Prins Albert*, did not make her approach to the berth until about 11 o'clock. While swinging off the berth she was caught by the wind on her port side, drifted sideways and ended up across the entrance of the old harbour with her stern on a mudbank and her bow resting on the west pier, lifting some granite blocks in the process. She remained in this position for about 20 minutes until the tug *Anglian Reiver* went to her aid but the strain of attempting to move the *Prins Filip* resulted in her engines overheating. The Dutch tug, the *Katherine W*, was trapped inside the harbour and also attempted to push the ferry away from the wall. Unfortunately, her engines were directed in the wrong direction and in the process the *Prins Filip* gained a dent in her hull. Eventually the Belgian ship managed to get her stern into the wind and

The Prins Filip *dwarfs the berth at Ramsgate Harbour in August 1996. (Mike Louagie)*

after 90 minutes berthed at No. 3 linkspan. After this inauspicious start, three days later she entered commercial service between Ostend and Ramsgate but it was not a happy relationship with the ever-present risk of grounding at low water.

January was to be a bad month for RMT with traffic figures down by some 40%, compared with the same period during 1993 operating out of Dover.

On 6th February, the jetfoil terminal finally arrived at Ramsgate from Dover's Admiralty Pier and the fast ferry operations commenced again six days later using the *Princesse Clementine* and *Prinses Stephanie*.

Two months later the Channel Tunnel opened its doors to traffic, which put further pressures on both Sally and RMT's operations out of Ramsgate.

Meanwhile in the light of the opening of the Channel Tunnel and internal operational problems, the German company Olau Line decided to withdraw their services from Sheerness to Vlissingen as from May. Following the announcement, Sally Line were quick to offer customers a replacement operation between Ramsgate and Vlissingen using the freighter *Sally Sun*. The chartered Sally Line freighter *Sally Eurobridge* (ex *Schiaffino*) was later brought in to support the 'Sun' on the new Dutch operation.

During May 1994, RMT carried satisfactory loadings for the first time since switching their Ostend-UK operations to Ramsgate in January. The number of passengers, mainly day-trippers, increased by 13% on figures of the previous year and coach traffic also increased although car and freight traffic still remained in decline.

The next couple of months were not to be a happy period for either the RMT service or Sally Line. On Thursday, 25th August, Sally's ferry

The Jetfoil Prinses Stephanie *pictured at the Jetfoil terminal (ex* Reine Astrid (I)*) at Ramsgate in August 1994. (Mike Louagie)*

The *Sally Star* and the *Prins Filip* pass each other mid-Channel whilst both Sally and Ostend Lines operated from Ramsgate Harbour. *(FotoFlite)*

Sally Star was inward-bound on a freight run from Dunkerque West when some eight miles off the Kentish port an explosion caused a serious fire in her engine room. The fire quickly took hold and smoke and flames could be seen from the shore. The vessel was evacuated and firemen were lifted in by helicopter to prevent the flames from spreading. Eventually the damage was contained and the *Sally Star* was sent off for repairs. The company lost no time in chartering the spare and unrefurbished *Princesse Marie-Christine* from their Belgian partners. She was to prove totally unsatisfactory for the route and was to cause more headaches over the next couple of months, until the 'Star' resumed service on 14th October.

The fire onboard the *Sally Star* was quickly overshadowed by the collapse of Ramsgate's new overhead walkway linking the terminal and No. 3 berth on the morning of 14th September. The final foot passengers were boarding the *Prins Filip* when without warning the first section of the covered walkway collapsed into the vehicle ramp, killing six people and injuring seven others. Immediately there was an investigation into the Swedish-built structure at the port. With this berth out of action, the Ostend operation had to be switched to No. 2, which was the Sally freight berth.

Meanwhile, Sally Line's freight service linking Ramsgate and Vlissingen was switched to Dartford in early October, using the *Sally Sun* and *Sally Eurobridge*. The service was supplemented in March 1995 by the entry into service of the *Sally Euroway* (ex *Argo*). Sally Line later claimed that the increase in demand for freight space on their new service between Dartford and Vlissingen had grown by some 120% since transferring the operation to the Thames in October. Following the arrival of the *Sally Euroway*, the *Sally Eurobridge* was withdrawn and later replaced by the chartered freighter *Purbeck*.

There were many who believed at this time that the future of all cross-Channel services (apart from Dover-Calais) lay in unaccompanied freight and as Dartford offered more potential for this trade than did Ramsgate, the move to the Thames port (adjacent to the M25) seemed to be justified.

The *Sally Star* inward bound from Dunkerque to Ramsgate. Following the demise of Sally Line the vessel was transferred to the Baltic. *(FotoFlite)*

The *Reine Astrid* and *Bazias 3* pass each other at the entrance to Ostend Harbour in July 1993. *(Mike Louagie)*

1995

The Belgian Government's decision to move the Ostend service to Ramsgate resulted in a disastrous first year's trading on the route which made a loss of BFr 2 billion - twice as much as it had lost when operating from Dover the previous year. The Belgians had failed to prepare themselves for the opening of the Channel Tunnel whereas their competitors had both improved standards and introduced their own 'shuttle services' on their respective Dover-Calais services. The attractiveness of the new Dover services and the improved quality of the 'turn up and go' operation that they now offered, combined with the Tunnel's own 'Shuttle' service, was to have a detrimental effect on all south coast cross-Channel operations from Ramsgate to Portsmouth. And the closer they were to Dover and the Tunnel, the worse the problem was exaggerated. Sally undoubtedly suffered as a result of the opening of the Tunnel with passenger and car numbers in decline, despite attractive offers for people to travel on their two-and-a-half hour route.

The future of the Ostend jetfoil service was also in doubt as from September 1995 as all international trains would be rescheduled to terminate at Brussels, instead of Ostend, from where passengers would be expected to cross to the UK by Eurostar.

In summer 1995 the Department of Transport rejected a further request to build a £21 million relief road into Ramsgate Harbour. This

The *Sally Euroroute* outward bound from Ostend. *(John Hendy)*

news came hard on the heels of the resignation in July of Michael Kingshott, who had led Sally Line from the start of its operations in 1981. Perhaps he had seen the writing on the wall at Ramsgate but he now joined John I. Jacobs who were to become the owners of Dart Line.

Mr. Bill Moses, formerly of Eurolink Ferries, Hoverspeed, Sealink and Olau, was appointed Chief Executive of Sally Line following the company's decision to concentrate on the Ramsgate routes. It is doubtful if there was anyone else with his breadth of experience of the cross-Channel trades and if Sally Line and Ramsgate were suffering from the magnetism exercised by both the Tunnel and Dover, Mr. Moses was certainly the man to find a solution to save them. A drastic re-think was required and in order to compete with the speed factor, as offered by his competitors, Mr. Moses stated that he intended to dramatically improve the sailing times between both Belgium and France by introducing fast ferries.

The company also revamped its image with a new logo and the adoption of the Silja Line seal's head on the hulls and funnels of the ships and both the *Sally Star* and *Sally Sky* received extensive refits.

RMT's traffic figures for 1995 were: 1,752,000 passengers (4% down on 1994), 239,000 cars (up 6%), 8,200 coaches (up 2%) and 82,000 freight units (up 16%) but with the Ostend service now in serious financial plight, on 27th October the Belgian Government appointed Mr. Ivo Radelet as the Crisis Manager of RMT, which had made a BEF3 billion loss over a BEF3.6 billion turnover in the previous year.

The following March, Mr Radelet presented his interim report confirming the company's future before the Belgium Parliamentary Committee of Transport. He stated in his report that the only way that RMT could survive was to opt for fast ferries in which minimum crews would be required. This fell nicely in line with Sally Line's long-term

The *Sally Euroway* makes her way up the Thames to the Dartford Terminal in October 1995. *(John Hendy)*

strategy as, under new management, as a matter of urgency they too were also looking to introduce fast craft on their Ramsgate-Dunkerque service.

1996

Sally Line's Dartford-Vlissingen freight operation duly passed into the ownership of the newly-formed Dart Line in early January 1996. Sally claimed at the time that there had been significant losses incurred on the Dartford-Vlissingen route due mainly to the start-up costs and from the fierce competition from Eurolink's new operation at Sheerness in place of Olau. The *Sally Euroway* remained on charter until the summer when the new operators introduced their own tonnage to replace her.

During spring 1996, Sally Line announced that they planned to have at least one fast craft in operation across the Channel by May 1997. The type of craft favoured at the time was a monohull construction. Such a craft would give vehicle capacity for about 200 and a passenger capacity for 800. Bill Moses stated that the fast craft technology could be used to split passenger and freight carryings and believed that this change was likely to grow as new safety legislation for existing conventional ferries pushed up costs and reduced operational flexibility. At the time, Sally felt that this move would allow them to avoid becoming a casualty of the opening of the Channel Tunnel.

On Friday 20th September, the Belgian Council of Ministers finally accepted RMT's drastic reorganisation plans. The long-established company was dismantled and formed into a new private company, which was originally known as Newco Pax, which would be owned two-thirds by the UK subsidiary of Australian Holyman Ltd and one-third by Silja. High-speed ferries, initially the *Condor 12*, would commence the operation the

The chartered freight vessel *Sally Euroroute* (ex *Bazias 3*) leaves Ostend for Ramsgate. *(Mike Louagie)*

e *Reine Astrid* laid up at Ostend in March 1995. *(John Hendy)*

The impressive-looking *Viking 6* at speed whilst on service between Ramsgate and Dunkerque. *(FotoFlite)*

following March. Two months later a second new 81 metre InCat craft, then on trials, would be added to the Ramsgate-Ostend operation. Crossing times would be reduced to 90 minutes, with two fast ferries in service and an eight-daily service would be offered in both directions. Both craft would be crewed by Belgians and 302 Belgian nationals would be offered jobs in the new company.

Sally Line later announced that it would further develop its freight-only service between Ostend and Ramsgate, replacing the *Sally Eurolink* and *Sally Euroroute* with the *Purbeck* and *Sally Euroway*. In addition to these ships, which both carried in excess of twelve drivers, a further ro-ro ship with a capacity for 80 trailers and 40 drivers would be added to the fleet at Ramsgate. With three freighters, offering six daily sailings in both directions, Sally hoped to fill the gap left by RMT as from 1st March 1997, the day after the RMT operation closed.

At the end of 1996, the *Sally Sky* was withdrawn from the service with the result of 150 personnel losing their jobs, mainly French catering crew

The *Prins Filip* berthed at Ramsgate prior to the last daylight sailing of RMT to Ostend. *(Miles Cowsill)*

This historic picture shows the three Ostend vehicle ferries, *Prins Albert*, *Princesse Marie-Christine* and *Prinses Maria-Esmeralda* following the demise of the Ramsgate-Ostend service. *(Mike Louagie)*

in addition to 52 engine room staff. At the time, the future of the *Sally Star* did not extend beyond November 1997, after which time she was due to return to her Swedish owners, Gotland Line.

During mid-December, the *Sally Sky* was given a thorough upgrading of her passenger facilities in preparation for her new freight role. The renamed vessel would operate as a ro-ro ship on Sally's Ostend route with the *Purbeck* and *Sally Euroway*. The *Sally Sky* was to operate on a reduced passenger certificate and was to be crewed by former RMT personnel. The main reason for retaining the vessel was that she would operate as a back-up to the fast craft operation of Holyman Sally.

1997

The Holyman Sally operation commenced on 1st March with the 81 metre InCat craft *Holyman Diamant* (ex *Condor 12*) operating a special trip to Belgium at the same time the *Holyman Rapide* (ex *Holyman Express*) took British media from the UK. The company aimed to carry 1.7 million passengers annually between Ostend and Ramsgate. It was stated that

The InCat craft *Holyman Diamant* outward bound from Ramsgate to Ostend during her first season on the route in May 1997. *(Mike Louagie)*

Sally's UK's own Ostend-Ramsgate freight service, which was quite independent of the Holyman-Sally service, would remain unaffected by the new operation at Ostend.

As a result of the reorganisation of the Ostend operations, 1,380 people lost their jobs and the RMT vessels were later disposed of by the Belgian Government. After holing herself in October 1996 the *Reine Astrid* had promptly been sold to Moby Ferries but half-sisters *Prins Albert* and the older *Princesse Marie-Christine* along with the superferry *Prins Filip* were sent to Dunkerque to lay-up while the twin jetfoils were 'mothballed' in Ostend. The first ship was duly purchased by Denval Marine, owners of the Slovenian operators TransEuropa Shipping Lines (TSL), and named *Eurovoyager*. The company eventually acquired the unrefurbished 'PMC' which they renamed *Primrose*.

After refitting at Tilbury, the *Sally Sky* emerged as the *Eurotraveller* for her Sally Freight Ramsgate-Ostend ro-ro service which she operated with the *Euroway* (ex *Sally Euroway*) and the *Purbeck*. Both ships were joined in May by the former *Rosebay* from the Harwich-Hook service, which was briefly renamed *Eurostar*, and then *Eurocruiser*, which replaced the *Purbeck* on the link.

Further expansion of Holyman Sally services came when it was announced that they were to start a new fast ferry service from Ramsgate to Dunkerque East using the smaller 74 metre craft *Condor 10*. The service was set up to attract mainly day-trippers as its operations were into the heart of the city of Dunkerque instead of out at Dunkerque West from where Sally had operated their services since 1981.

Meanwhile, the traditional Sally link between Ramsgate and

The Sally freight vessel *Eurostar* (ex *Rosebay*) leaves Ostend for Ramsgate in May 1997. *(Philippe Holthof)*

The *Euroway* and *Eurovoyager* pass each other in mid-Channel. *(FotoFlite)*

The mainstay of the Ramsgate-Dunkerque service for many years were the *Sally Sky* and *Sally Star*. Both vessels are seen here in mid-Channel prior to the jumboisation of the *Sally Sky*. (FotoFlite)

The much-travelled *Euroway* (ex *Argo*) is seen here in blue and white livery prior to the application of the Sally logo to her hull. *(Mike Louagie)*

This morning view shows the *Prins Albert* in her original Ostend Line livery and the newly-renamed *Wisteria* (ex *Prinses Maria-Esmeralda*) in her new owner's livery. *(Mike Louagie)*

The much travelled *Purbeck* is seen whilst on charter to Sally Line. *(Mike Louagie)*

This view shows the last departure of the *Princesse Marie-Christine* from Ostend prior to her layup and pending sale at Dunkerque on 18th April 1997. *(Mike Louagie)*

The *Eurostar* is seen here berthed at the doubledeck linkspan originally built for the *Prins Filip*. Behind the vessel can be seen the railway station. *(Mike Louagie)*

Dunkerque West closed on Sunday 13th April, the *Sally Star* departing from the Thanet port three days later.

The 74 metre *Condor 10* took up service for Holyman Sally on 15th May but the operation was only to be short-lived and on 29th September it was announced that the Dunkerque East service was to be axed as soon as practicable. This turned out to be almost immediately and it promptly closed with the 22.00 from Dunkerque on 3rd October. It was believed that after the short operating season of six months, the losses on both the Ostend and Dunkerque fast ferry operations amounted to some £8 million.

The company announced in the autumn that they were now going to focus all their resources on the Ostend route on which they claimed to have opened up a new day trip and short break market since it had started in the March. Sally Freight (still Silja Line owned) meanwhile would continue to establish their operations to Ostend and had not ruled out a return to Dunkerque West at some time in the future. However, at the end of the year, further bad news came with both partners announcing further

The *Holyman Rapide* arriving at Ostend in October 1997. *(Philippe Holthof)*

The *Condor 10* arriving at Dunkerque East in August 1997. *(John Hendy)*

substantial losses on their respective operations. Holyman Ltd were also facing serious financial problems at home in Australia and also with their joint venture on the UK Channel Islands services. The time was due for some form of retrenchment and in a final effort to create a success of their substantial investments, by the end of the year Holyman were being lured by a new partner to run their Ostend operation.

1998

Sea Containers' subsidiary Hoverspeed signed an agreement with Holyman Ltd, Silja OY and the Belgian Government providing for the takeover of a 50% shareholding in Holyman Sally Ltd and to supply management for the company's UK-Belgium passenger and car services. The reconstituted company was named Hoverspeed Holyman Ltd and both parties agreed to provide £1.25 million working capital for the new

The fast craft *Holyman Rapide* and the *Holyman Diamant* together at Ostend. *(Mike Louagie)*

group. The new operation concentrated on the historic RMT route from Dover-Ostend. The Chairman of Holyman Ltd, Mr Richard Austin, said, "It is no secret that Holyman Sally Ltd has been unprofitable on the Ostend-Ramsgate route. Dover is the largest ferry port in the world and has a considerable drawing power because of its easy road access. Hoverspeed is able to accommodate our ships at its existing ferry terminal in the Western Docks at Dover and to manage the company's business at a marginal cost."

During 1997, Holyman Sally had carried 1.2 million passengers and 220,000 cars on its Ramsgate-Ostend route. It is interesting to note that shortly after the announcement of the joint venture David Benson of Sea Containers said, "Back in 1996 we proposed to the Belgian Government the very service between Dover and Ostend that we are starting on 6th March."

The final Holyman Sally Ostend-Ramsgate sailing was the 20.00 on 5th March with the last from Ramsgate timed at 21.45.

The following day the *Holyman Diamant* left Ostend at 08.00 with 193 passengers on the first commercial crossing to Dover since 31st January 1993.

The departure of Holyman from Ramsgate brought both anger and despair. The Labour MP for South Thanet was quoted as saying, "Holyman made it a clear commitment to the town and the area and a lot of projects have been started on the back of this. They don't seem to have had any concept of responsibilities they took on or the commitments that they made because of their business. I am inclined to say good riddance to them."

Meanwhile the new Port Ramsgate Chairman, Mr Bill Moses, revealed that he had received at least two tentative approaches from other ferry operators. In spite of the doom and gloom at Ramsgate, Sally Freight claimed that their Ramsgate-Ostend freight business had grown by some 20% during the past year and Kent County Council confirmed that Holyman's withdrawal from the port would not affect the construction of the new £30 million, 1.4 mile port approach road which was due to open in 2000.

More bad news was looming when it was reported in the 'Financial Times' in February 1998 that Sally's parent company Silja planned to sell off their loss-making subsidiaries of Port Ramsgate and Sally Freight.

But two months later Sally announced that they planned to open a new passenger service to Ostend which would trade under the banner of Sally Direct. This represented a final effort to reverse the ailing fortunes of Sally UK and was to be a day and night service launched to capitalise on the summer season and feature a turn-up and go facility for day-trippers and motorists. The 'direct' theme was to run throughout the operation with bookings being made directly with the operator and duty-free goods coming direct from the factory with substantial discounts being offered and prices rounded down to the nearest pound.

Mr. Bill Moses, Chief Executive of Sally Direct, said "Because this will not be a large operation, we will be able to offer a friendly, personal high-quality service to travellers. The people of Thanet have made it clear how valuable the passenger service is to them and their business and we have launched this service in direct response to local demand. We are relying on the community around us to give the service its full support." Mr. Moses added that the initial targets for carryings were modest and stressed that the service would be a starting point for what he hoped would be a return to a full passenger service from Ramsgate. His ambition at the time was that the port might offer a capacity carrying of 5,000,000 passengers a year.

The *Condor 10* pictured at Ramsgate in October 1997 following the closure of the fast ferry service between Ramsgate and Dunkerque East. *(Miles Cowsill)*

The *Eurotraveller* was timed to sail at 01.00 and 12.00 (Mondays to Fridays) in addition to an 08.00 sailing at weekends from Ramsgate. Return sailings from Ostend were scheduled at 07.30 and 20.15 (weekdays) and 17.00 at weekends. The service commenced on 20th May 1998.

On the first sailing of the *Eurotraveller*, some 200 passengers who disembarked onto the quayside at Ostend were allowed to go no further by Belgian Immigration officials and Harbour Police. They stated that as Britain had not signed up to the Schengen Agreement, which governs passenger movement through the European Union, passengers would not be allowed ashore. The saga turned into a public relations nightmare with both the Chief Executive, Bill Moses, his guests and passengers having to return on the ship to Kent.

A spokesman for the company stated that Sally had been given to understand that all the necessary conditions and authorities to disembark passengers were in force. The fact that, with the backing of the Government, rival UK-Belgium Hoverspeed Holyman had certain operational rights over large areas of the dockside at Ostend, could have served as a further reason why a second passenger operation was unwelcome.

May 1998 also saw the end of the *Eurocruiser's* charter and her return to the Hook - Harwich link when she resumed the name *Rosebay*. In her place came the *Eurovoyager*, the former RMT vessel *Prins Albert*, which made a totally unexpected return to the port for which she was built and which she had closed for the Belgian Government at the end of February 1997.

The Sally Direct passenger service finally commenced on 29th July after the Belgian authorities had granted permission for the *Eurotraveller* to land passengers at Ostend berth 4 but apart from at weekends, the service still failed to attract the traffic levels required to make it profitable and the ship's limited freight capacity made it difficult to plan for further growth. With the fierce competition both at Dover and through the Channel Tunnel, the news finally came on 5th November that in an effort to reverse

Handling Services and the Port of Ostend, commenced operations without so much as missing a single sailing. The *Eurovoyager* continued working after the demise of Sally Line and made her first arrival for TransEuropa Shipping Lines berthing at 04.00 from Ostend on 21st November.

Some five days later, the company introduced their ro-ro freighter *Juniper* on the link. The *Primrose* (ex *Princesse Marie-Christine*) was added in June 1999 and on 27th August 2000 the *Larkspur* (ex *Eurotraveller, Sally Sky, Viking 2*) returned to Ramsgate in her fourth incarnation spanning a 14 year association with the port.

The long awaited £30 million Harbour Approach Road was finally opened on 30th June 2000.

There has also been speculation concerning a new passenger operation to Ostend from Ramsgate but to date nothing has become of it.

The *Prinses Stephanie* leaves Ostend on trials with potential buyers as Hoverspeed's *Rapide* is at the berth pending her departure to Dover. *(Mike Louagie)*

their trading losses of the previous year, Neptun Maritime (the Silja Line parent company) had decided to concentrate on their core Baltic business and that the English Channel operations were to be sold off.

At midnight on 20th November 1998 the Sally Direct and Sally Freight links with Ostend both came to an end. The *Eurotraveller* was withdrawn and laid-up for sale in Dunkerque and in the following year was sold to Denval Marine (who renamed her *Larkspur*) for further operations within their fleet.

The Port of Ramsgate and its connections with Belgium did not die after the withdrawal of Sally Line. As Ramsgate New Port, it returned to the hands of Thanet Council, which in turn allowed a new operator to start a freight service to Ostend. The Slovenian company, TransEuropa Shipping Lines, with its partners H R Services Ltd., Diaz Haulage, Ostend Cargo

The Cypriot registered *Eurovoyage*r (ex *Prins Albert*) makes an impressive view in rough conditions en-route to Ostend. *(FotoFlite)*

44

The *Eurotraveller* arrives at Ostend in her Holyman Sally Ferries livery. *(Mike Louagie)*

High water at Ostend as the Sally Star makes her way between the pier heads bound for Ramsgate. (Mike Louagie)

A Sally Retrospect

The 17 year history of Sally Line in all its different guises was a brave initiative to provide the public with an alternative way of crossing the English Channel.

In its early years the company thrived simply because it was different offering cut-price crossings, a bright and clean Scandinavian style and standards and bright red ships. The first element attracted an 'economy' corner of the tourist market and during the summer months the passenger list would be swelled by large numbers of day-excursionists from the Thanet resorts. The escape which the service offered from the hectic fast lane of Dover - Calais was welcomed by many but road connections to Ramsgate remained poor while they improved to such an extent along the northern French coast that Dunkerque West and Calais became but a short drive and there was little or nothing to be gained timewise by arriving at 'Port Rapide.'

Port Ramsgate was always hampered by a lack of infrastructure (which in one way or another continued to plague the Sally service throughout its 17 years and was only eased after the company's demise). A further problem was the failure of its Scandinavian owners to provide it with ships which a) would remain on the route for longer than a season at a time and b) which reflected the changing trends and standards in cross-Channel travel that took place in preparation for the opening of the Channel Tunnel. It was not simply a case of the survival of the fittest but the survival of the operators who were able to adapt most successfully to the changes forced upon them. And to be able to do that required a strong financial backing which Sally's owners were ultimately unable to sustain.

Dispite local willingness and effort to make them succeed, the late attempts to provide both a fast ferry service and latterly a cut-price 'Direct' link with the Continent, the former was badly conceived and marketed whilst the latter may possibly have been viewed by the owners as a final effort to generate revenue from surplus tonnage. Ultimately,

Booming Ramsgate Harbour in April 1990 with the *Sally Star* and *Sally Sky* at their berths. *(Chris Randall)*

however, commercial pressures forced the closure of the service.

For many of the 17 years under review, the operation of the Sally service was a struggle against ship owners, financial backers, local authorities, competitors, the Channel Tunnel, changing traffic trends and customer expectations.

With the right ships on the right service at the right time coupled with a longer-term willingness and commitment on the part of the company's owners, then things could have turned out differently.

There is no doubt that the passing of Sally left a significant gap in the market which others moved hastily to fill. Theirs was an honest endeavour against mounting odds to provide something which was different. Tremendous efforts were made in the UK to keep the operation afloat but in the last analysis, the final decision lay elsewhere.

For the last thirteen years we have produced over 50 books covering ferry operations in the UK and Europe, and are the leading specialists in the history of the ferry industry and current ferry operations. Ferry Publications also produce a quality ferry magazine **"European Ferry Scene"** which is accepted as Europe's leading ferry journal.

Our most recent titles and forthcoming books include:

Ferries 2001 - British Isles and Northern Europe Edition

Ferries 2001 - Southern Europe Edition*

Sea Containers - The Fleet*

The Townsend Eight*

In Fair Weather and in Foul

Caledonian MacBrayne - The Fleet

A Century of North-West European Ferries

P&O - The Fleet

Greek Ferries

*Published during 2001

For more information or a copy of the current booklist please contact us at:

Ferry Publications, PO Box 33, Ramsey, Isle of Man, IM99 4LP

Tel: +44 (0) 1624 898445   Fax: +44 (0) 1624 898449

email: ferrypubs@aol.com   website: www.ferrypubs.co.uk